# LE RÊVE…THE DREAM

*Poems and prose inspired by my life with Cooper*

## by Lisa Crivello

I've Been Licked Books®
1417 Del Paso Blvd #164
Sacramento . CA 95815
www.ivebeenlicked.com

First published by I've Been Licked Books® 9.1.2024

ISBN: 978-0-9891393-9-7

Printed in the United States of America

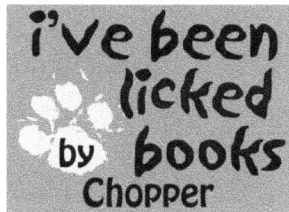

# For Cooper

She lived her life to the melody that was always playing in the background of her mind; one she thought to be her greatest masterpiece because it was created from all the experiences and events that made her. The melody would continue to play intermittently throughout her present life. It was a somber yet heartfelt tune, much like the sentimentality that seemed to follow her.

It was like time stood still in many ways. After her beloved mother's passing, she had felt life's events much more deeply. She missed the love that she received from her mother, the deep bond that they shared. She was told that she no longer smiled as she once did, like in pictures with her mother. She took notice, and that realization is ever present. She would strive to recreate that feeling, that love that created that smile throughout her life; always being let down.

She knew the meaning of unconditional love, the kind her mother had portrayed. Her whole existence was built upon it and she tried to exhibit that through the constructs of her own life. She would find people who would prey upon this and take it for weakness. Being too caught up in the search to feel what she had once had with her mother, she would not see the reality of people and their flaws. See, her mother was angelic, perfect, graceful, empathetic and compassionate beyond measure, traits that she longed so badly for, and seemed to be lacking in her world.

Through her search, walls were created and decisions made. From there on out, she started to feel isolated as the world couldn't live up to her confounds. Everyone let her down, including her husband, who had chosen his love for drugs over her. She was devastated, she thought she had found love only to be disappointed.

The one good thing that came out of the marriage that renewed her faith in love was a little Shihtzu/Maltese mix, whom she would name Cooper. He was unconditional love himself, she would find that he would be her greatest companion, and help her regain her interest and joy in life again. Although not perfect, Cooper has taught her to feel and smile like she once had when her mother was alive. All he wanted was to be loved, and she supplied that more than ever.

Cooper was lifechanging...and so began Le Rêve -The Dream.

# The two who made me had to leave

Only compilations remain
In a tear stained background of disdain
I'm traveling back through the clouds and mire
to find my soul in its finest hour,
it's been way too long since the laughter engulfed me
way too long without memories…
I am an ongoing dedication
to the sky above
who carry my loves
and the sun that rises
and outlines time,
there you will always exist in my mind…

## *For Susan*

Our times were special
Watching the candle
Drinking cold brew
Thinking we knew
Escaping reality too…
Intoxicating Adventures
Dangerous Transgressions
Concerts
Parties
Timbuktu
Evolving with time
Firming our bond
You, me
Me, You
Us two…

# Dreamscape

Green weeds of summer,
weave in and out of each other gracefully,
while images sustain memories of previous summers.
Lying in fields of wild flowers, carelessly surrounded in color –
The weeds blowing up against my skin,
generating a laughter from within.
As they continue to glow-sharply, making their pattern.
My journey had already begun…

————————/\\/\\/\\—————————

# The Gift Box

It's sound draws us near
After the door is opened
Emotion defines a clear
Illusion through sight
Taking us beyond depth
We never knew –
A yet deeper sense of existence
Become known.
We are never the same…

# For JR

Things were never the same
The neighborhood had changed
When dad sold the house
One thing stayed the same
The smile on my face
When I saw my momma's name

We all grow up and go our ways
But sooner or later we gotta face
Memories, yea they may fade
But love in the heart
Always, always, remains...

They say time heals all wounds
I don't think that's true
Time is different to me
And to you
In life dreams come true
There's a God cuz he brought me you...

*Dedicated to my mother,*
*my best friend & confidant forever*

A Question Please

How are we to know

Timeless Moments

Never let them

Go –

Waiting 4 a sign

Basing life on

Time –

It's not that easy

She said,

You won't ever

Know

You'll just have to

Be

The 1 led –

A choice
Will come,
How are we to know
Life is a path
And so you grow
Things unfair, unseen
Unknown
All the while
Alone, alone
Left to wonder
Why –
The meaning is not clearly shown.
Different moods
Changing like
The setting sun
Never want to
Let go –

## Fallen Star

The night opened up
And the sky poured in
The shadow bands were glowing
From within.
Starlit sky's falling like
Never ending signs
Elude my mind…

─────────────/\/\/\─────────────

## Film

Unabashed

clever

Cunning

You taught

Me so

Much

We were winning

Time didn't

Matter

Like diamonds glistening

On the water

We will never shatter

Memories stay

in the mind

Like

everlasting glue

in me just us two..

You were always you

─────────────/\/\/\─────────────

# Greg

So many colors
yet unexposed
You're a bright light head to toe
You inspired with all you know
never letting your colors go
Your impact is forever
too bad
you couldn't have known
I keep you in color
always visible
In my mind
And in my soul
music kept you, savior unknown
You lived it
And shared it
A true blessing to behold
You will forever stay
my beautiful friend
for you will never end

July 28,1968 - July 26, 2020

## *She*

Listening to the rain
a feeling comes over me,
Seeing your face in places unknown
feels comfortable, feels like home.
You enter in my dreams,
silent and aloof
Slide out without
even the slightest clue
Not knowing
if I'll ever find truth.

Light comes through my window
Pale and blue,
tears in my mind
Still searching for you.

Listening to the rain,
dancing puddles of excitement
entangled in chaos
Allows freedom from remorse.
Sighing comfortably,
I have the Lord.

## Guitar

He strummed relaxing, with extreme emotion, lost in a tune
for which his instrument was soon to take over.
The Guitar

## The Desk

The wood grains saturated with emotions
of previous desk dwellers, only to endure more
resides hopelessly in wonder of its next test of age.

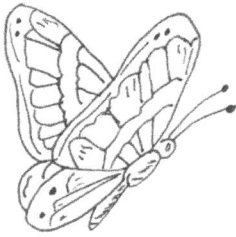

# Kira

Sifting through the rubble
You find your winding down
With every step
your lifted
Above the ground
No time and space
No hate no waste
Your love carries you
Ever present ever true
You leave your mark
Forever YOU...

For Kira 11/14/18

# Cadence

Things ever changing
ever present
Tormenting effervescence
All the while
fascinating clues
Cannot be
determined by you.
You there
Not there,
uncertain
certain
To be told
Close curtain...

# *Boundless*

Search the path for redemption, make no exception,
allow no interruptions for life is salvation...
I lift my hand to the sky, felt you outpour into my mind,
forever intwined.
I'm safe there within your presence, solace and grace
for there is no heaven in this place.
I want to be where you are,
I lift my heart to you
all sacred, all brand new.
Forever in your grace
I take refuge in this place,
hiding but fully seen
life is not as it seems.
You keep a watchful eye,
always have
Omnipresent in my mind's sky.
To be with you, still to come
Wait though
It is not done.

---/\/\/\---

## To "D"

Sensations flow
Through my gaze
I write
Carefully and slow –
Feeling good
that's my mood –
at least for now
Haven't written in a while
maybe that's cause
for my smile –
I pick up the pen
and watch the ink
dance –
It's the only thing that
can put my feelings in synch –
Haven't been inspired
As of yet –
life has had me tired
but I won the bet –

---/\/\/\---

Does it flow
Does he know
only time will tell
until then I must reap
what I sow –
A song, a poem
A way of self expression
time to show meaning
and tone
But not the only way to make an impression –
Is it trivial?
Or menial?
Possibly so
But how is one to know…

# Waikiki, Oahu

Sky's blue, only time will tell
Cloud flutter from above
A wondrous kind of love.
Mountains too high to climb,
Memories of what's left
Behind.
Only to sit and ponder
What's on the other
Side?
Oceans deep and
Mystical
My mind seeks for answers,
but is still left skeptical.
The watch on my arm,
Ticking away
The time
Couldn't stop
To be kind
Sometimes, feels
Like a crime…

## *Frozen in Time*

A smile encapsulated
For that moment
Stood still
Reeling from years together
Still so new
Immense love
Saved by you
Everyday thankful
Everyday anew
Adventures found
In eyes brown
We three inseparable
Forever found
Your love knows no end
And so you will stay
A smile today

# The House of Intimidating Objects

And so it seemed that ages had passed while sitting in the
house of intimidating objects, this had to stop I must be heard.
To do this I would proceed aggressively and unstoppably
letting my oppressors know that I would not be an easy
opponent. I walked over to one of the objects,
hesitantly at first, my feet grew heavier and heavier
on approach, it felt as though cement had been
poured into the souls of my shoes.
My mind and eyes fought back and overcame the fear.

I now picked up the object, gazing at it in great wonder?
How could something so beautiful be so intimidating?!!
I did not have the answers, I was left in wonder,
and I wanted to use the object
My efforts won't stop there, here I go,
proceeding to use what I already know,
and of course to further my knowledge.
Amazingly enough, it happened for me
I wasn't regretting my choice of objects at all.
To be strict I was, and now
I would challenge all the other intimidating objects in the room.
There was just no stopping me now,
for I know the true feeling of –
just then the object found its trap, I was caught…
as an awful buzzing echoed and faintly disappeared.

I was intimidated once again, was I to stop trying
for fear that it would strike again or that I may fail?
No, I'll press on.
I'll be true to myself, I will master your secrets!
I had spoken too soon about challenging all the
other intimidating objects in the room,
only to be trapped by a message in disguise
to the overconfident me!
In this house the guitar taught me to be true to myself,
I continued with extreme caution…

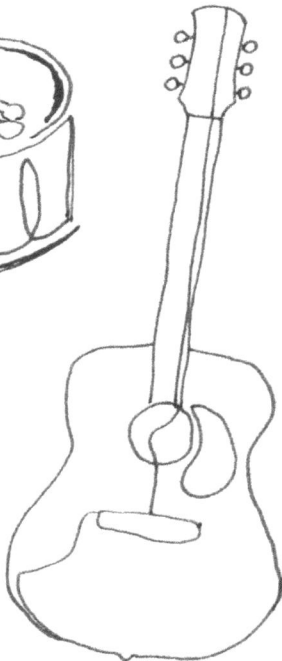

# *Looking Glass*

It shows an outside appearance looking in,
Not just features alone,
But history explaining where they've been.
Insights into ancestry
Through a face which beheld
Merely humanity.
Yes, peering into the looking glass
There was future to be lived and learned
It was then decided, things must change
As to which direction the journey
would begin,
and desire burned…

———————/\/\/\———————

# *For Sherry*

The words were still flowing,
As she gasped for air
Closed her mouth
And smiled
Finishing tediously
A masterpiece in itself…

# Under the Canopy of Oaks

I breathed you in
I looked up and felt you there
You, me, we
In that moment the whistling trees
Scattered bits of sky
Unbridled a sign
Faded in and out
Of mind
You are present
Listening
Appearing
Changing
Standing still
Peace is now
Leaves drop
Awaken my soul
Time passes
Let it go…

www.ingramcontent.com/pod-product-compliance
Lightning Source LLC
Chambersburg PA
CBHW042103060426
42446CB00046B/3472